D1709924

Grandmother's Cherry Cake

by

Janice (Taylor) Peek

DORRANCE
PUBLISHING CO
EST. 1920
PITTSBURGH, PENNSYLVANIA 15238

The contents of this work, including, but not limited to, the accuracy of events, people, and places depicted; opinions expressed; permission to use previously published materials included; and any advice given or actions advocated are solely the responsibility of the author, who assumes all liability for said work and indemnifies the publisher against any claims stemming from publication of the work.

All Rights Reserved
Copyright © 2020 by Janice (Taylor) Peek

No part of this book may be reproduced or transmitted, downloaded, distributed, reverse engineered, or stored in or introduced into any information storage and retrieval system, in any form or by any means, including photocopying and recording, whether electronic or mechanical, now known or hereinafter invented without permission in writing from the publisher.

Dorrance Publishing Co
585 Alpha Drive
Pittsburgh, PA 15238
Visit our website at *www.dorrancebookstore.com*

ISBN: 978-1-4809-9134-7
eISBN: 978-1-4809-9392-1

Thank you to my family and friends for their support. This is a true story in my childhood. The character names have been changed and are fictional except for PeeWee.

Place: Adams St. Northside of Pittsburgh, PA

Time: Summer 1963

Scene: Grandmother's Kitchen

Characters: Grandmother aka Holly, baby Aunt Dee Dee, baby Uncle Calvin, cousin Snowy Pops, baby cousin Marshmallow, my mom, Juicy, my baby brother, Tanker, and myself, PeeWee.

I live in a neighborhood of Pittsburgh, PA, called Oakland. My mom Juicy, my little brother, Tanker, and I live in a house up on a hill called Mackey St. Behind our house is a big mountain and it has a forest and seven neighbors. To get to the top or the bottom, we have to walk up or down city steps. The easy way to get around is to go to Bates Street. You can drive or walk, up or down this long street. It is a very curvy and winding road that looks like a giant snake to me!

My mom said, "PeeWee and Tanker come on, I am taking both of you to Grandmother Holly's house." I was six years old and my brother, Tanker is four years old; we were both so excited. We were jumping up and down, screaming, and laughing with joy!

To get to Grandmother's house, we traveled by car to the Northside of Pittsburgh, to the neighborhood of Manchester, where Grandmother lives. We have to cross bridges over the Allegheny River. As we sat in the car, Tanker and I looked out the left side of the car window. We saw the Monongahela River and on the mountainside is a trolley car on a track going straight up the side of the mountain to the top of Mt. Washington. "Wow! That looks funny." We thought the trolley car was going to fall down the mountain into the river.

We arrived at Grandmother's house on Adams Street. Tanker and I jumped out of the car and ran into the kitchen to give Grandmother a big hug. We always had fun at Grandmother Holly's house. She did not always do things the way everyone else did, but she was special and funny and we loved her.

Her house always had a lot of people around, because Grandmother Holly had twelve children and many grandchildren.

This Saturday, it was only the young ones around, my baby Aunt Dee Dee, my baby Uncle Calvin. They are only four and three years old. My brother Tanker, some of my cousins - Snowy Pops who is three years old and Marshmall who is a ten month old baby. And I was there too!

PeeWee, Snowy Pop, Tanker, and Marshmallow are funny names for girls and a boy, but they have been our nicknames since we were little babies. Our family still calls us by our nicknames. The nicknames will never outgrow us. Ha, ha, ha! Smile!

After everybody's parent(s) left, Grandmother Holly
said, "What are we going to do today?"

We all said, "I don't know, Grandmother."

Grandmother Holly said, "How about I bake a cherry
cake."

We all hollered, "Yeah!" She checked her cupboards
and did not find the cherry cake mix.

"PeeWee," Grandmother said, "You are the oldest grandchild here today. I need you to go to the store and the buy the cherry cake mix."

I said, "Okay, Grandmother, I am ready to go."

Boy! All of us kids were so excited; we were jumping, hollering, laughing, and playing. We were so happy, because Grandmother Holly was going to bake us a cherry cake. Grandmother Holly gave me money and a note for the cherry cake mix. I ran happily out the door as fast as I could towards the corner store. The faster I could get to the store to buy the cake mix, the faster I could get back to Grandmother's house. I ran into the house yelling, "I got the cherry cake mix, Grandmother!"

Grandmother Holly took the box of cake mix and started reading the directions on the back of the box. She said, "Ummmmmmh! The directions say to use eggs. PeeWee, check the refrigerator, do we have eggs?" I went to refrigerator, opened the door and looked for the eggs.

I answered, "No, Grandmother, there are no eggs."

She said, "Okay," and started reading the directions again. Grandmother said, "PeeWee, check the refrigerator for milk." I opened the refrigerator and looked inside.

I answered, "No, Grandmother, there is no milk."

All of the kids got quiet and began to look so sad. I said," Grandmother, if we don't have any eggs and no milk, how can we make the cherry cake?"

Grandmother Holly said, "Don't worry, it takes more than no eggs and no milk to beat Grandmother Holly!"

Can you guess how we got our cherry cake?

Reader Pause

(Ask listeners to guess how

Grandmother Holly made a cherry cake.)

All of the children sat at the kitchen table, waiting patiently for Grandmother to finish her masterpiece. Grandmother Holly took out an iron skillet and put it on a top burner on the kitchen stove to heat up. She put the cake mix into a bowl, poured water into it, and began to stir. She put butter into the hot skillet. Grandmother Holly fried the cherry cake mix into pancakes. We all enjoyed those pancakes. That was the best cherry cake I ever had!

The End

CPSIA information can be obtained
at www.ICGtesting.com
Printed in the USA
BVHW020114171120
593477BV00003B/8